JILL S. POLLACK

SHIRLEY CHISHOLM

**FRANKLIN WATTS**
New York / Chicago / London / Toronto / Sidney
**A FIRST BOOK**

Frontispiece: Shirley Chisholm's senior picture from the
1946 *Broeklundian*, Brooklyn College's Yearbook.
Cover illustration by Gil Ashby

Photographs copyright ©: Brooklyn College, Special Collections: pp. 2, 21; Photo
Researchers, Inc./Andy Levin: p. 8; Archive Photos, NYC: pp. 12, 14 (Rising), 38;
Brooklyn Historical Society: pp. 16, 18; UPI/Bettmann Newsphotos: pp. 24, 28,
33, 41, 51, 56, 58; AP/Wide World Photos: pp. 30, 35, 43, 46, 48, 54.

Library of Congress Cataloging-in-Publication Data

Pollack, Jill S.
Shirley Chisholm / by Jill S. Pollack.
p. cm. — (A First book)
Includes bibliographical references and index.
ISBN 0-531-20168-6
1. Chisholm, Shirley, 1924– —Juvenile literature.
2. Legislators—United States—Biography—Juvenile literature.
3. Afro-Americans—Biography—Juvenile literature. 4. Presidential candidates—
United States—Biography—Juvenile literature. 5. Teachers—United States—
Biography—Juvenile literature. 6. United States. Congress.
House—Biography—Juvenile literature. [1. Chisholm, Shirley, 1924– .
2. Legislators. 3. Afro-Americans—Biography. 4. Women—Biography.]
I. Title. II. Series.
E840.8.C48P65 1994
328.73'092—dc20                                    93-31175
[B]                                                CIP AC

# CONTENTS

TO CARRIE

*Barbados, a small, rocky island in the Caribbean, was a place of love and learning for Shirley St. Hill during her years on her grandmother's farm.*

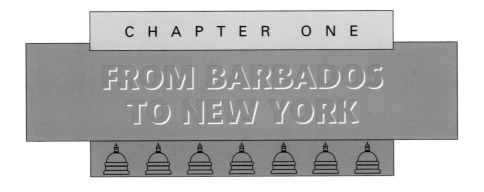

# CHAPTER ONE

# FROM BARBADOS TO NEW YORK

**BARBADOS,** a small island in the West Indies, was home to Shirley Anita St. Hill, who had lived on her grandmother's farm for seven years. Her grandmother, Mrs. Emily Seale, was a strict but loving person who began the lifelong education of this young girl who would grow up to run for president of the United States.

Shirley's father, Charles St. Hill, and her mother, Ruby Seale, were both part of a group of Barbadians that immigrated to Brooklyn in the 1920s. It was in Brooklyn that Charles and Ruby fell in love, married, and raised four daughters: Shirley was born in 1924, and her three sisters, Odessa, Muriel, and Selma, followed over the next several years.

When Shirley was three, her parents decided it

would be best for her and her sisters to go stay with Grandmother Seale in Barbados, where there would be room to run and play. If the children stayed with the grandmother for a few years, the St. Hills, who worked very hard, could save enough money to bring the girls back to New York and provide a house and proper education for them.

Grandmother Seale's farm was a wonderful place and full of new discoveries for Shirley, her sisters, and their four cousins, who also lived on the farm. There was no electricity or running water so the children had many chores. Their reward, however, was to run to the beach and play in the crisp, clear waters of the Caribbean.

Education has been a major theme in Shirley's life, and the first formalized education she had was in a one-room school in Barbados. Between the stern teachers and Grandmother Seale, Shirley became an excellent student who enjoyed her studies. She learned to read when she was only four years old and spent evenings huddled near a kerosene lamp to read her schoolbooks until Grandmother Seale pushed her off to bed.

On the island, Shirley was surrounded by love; the villagers were like one big family, welcoming Shirley and her cousins. She also developed a deep sense of pride that was nurtured first by Grandmother Seale, and later by Mr. and Mrs. St. Hill.

In 1934, Shirley's carefree life changed forever when the St. Hills decided it was time to bring their daughters home to Brooklyn. Upon their return to New York, Shirley and her sisters encountered a world vastly different from the slow and sunny days in Barbados. Compared to her grandmother's farm, Brooklyn was a cold and confusing place, where Shirley often got lost in the winding streets of her neighborhood.

The people who lived in Brooklyn in 1934 were mostly white, Jewish immigrants, and first-generation Americans. The St. Hill family was one of the few black families in the neighborhood, but the difference in skin color didn't seem to matter and, for the most part, everyone in Brooklyn got along.

The St. Hills lived in a "railroad flat," and like the cars on a train, the rooms were all in a line, requiring one to walk through each room to get to the next. In the wintertime, the apartment was barely heated by the one coal stove in the kitchen, and on some days the St. Hill girls stayed in bed just to keep warm.

Shirley's father worked in a bakery and came home at night to eat dinner with the family, read his beloved books and newspapers, and talk about poli-

*After Shirley and her sisters moved back to New York, they lived in Brooklyn. This is how the neighborhood looked in the 1940s when Shirley attended high school there.*

tics and social issues. Shirley absorbed her father's love of intellectual discussion and his thirst for knowledge. She remained very close to her father until his death and relished his love of debate and intellectual pursuits.

Mr. St. Hill's friends, also West Indian immigrants, would often gather at the St. Hill's apartment and enjoy late night discussions and debates about their island homes and racial politics. As the men sat around the kitchen table drinking and talking until late in the evening about the bigotry they faced because they were black, Shirley would lie awake in the next room craning her neck to hear the discussion. These midnight lessons would stay with Shirley for the rest of her life.

Shirley and her sisters were among the few black students in their school but the more obvious difference between them and their schoolmates was religion. While the St. Hills girls teased their Jewish neighbors about having to pray on Saturday, they got their fair share when Mrs. St. Hill paraded them through the streets to attend church — three times every Sunday.

Mrs. St. Hill was a very religious woman and believed in raising her children in a very strict and disciplined manner. How else would they learn to expect only the best from themselves, and how else would they learn to achieve all that they could!

This time in Shirley's life was during the Great Depression, when businesses and individuals suffered financial failure and unemployment was widespread. In Shirley's family, Mr. St. Hill found it necessary to accept jobs where he earned less money, and Mrs. St. Hill decided there was no choice but to

*Because the Great Depression brought tough economic conditions, many black women became domestics, or housekeepers, for white families in order to bring home some income.*

begin working as a domestic (or housekeeper) for white families in an area far from Brooklyn. Because she was not able to be home for her children, Mrs. St. Hill put Shirley in charge of Muriel, Odessa, and Selma and taught her the very important lesson of responsibility.

In 1936, the family moved to a larger apartment in the Bedford-Stuyvesant neighborhood of Brooklyn. Here Shirley began learning about prejudice and what it meant to be black in America. Her racial consciousness was beginning to develop, and in the years to come, Shirley would spend her career fighting racism and prejudice.

Because many black families moved to New York from the South during the Great Depression, the population of the Bedford-Stuyvesant area grew to be about 50 percent black in the 1940s. The neighborhood had been predominantly white, and these people fought to retain control of everything they could, from politics to building inspections. The newcomers were quite poor for the most part, and the white landlords and city inspectors took advantage of them at every turn. Black workers were routinely the last to be hired and the first to be fired as racism and bigotry grew.

This was the beginning of what many people later called the inner city. The black workers had to crowd

*Downtown Brooklyn was quite a contrast from Barbados for the St. Hill girls.*

into small parts of the city while white families remained in mostly white suburbs. This was an important time in Shirley's life, for it was here, in Bed-Stuy, that she learned firsthand of American racism.

**SHIRLEY** excelled in school and in 1942 graduated from Girls' High, one of the best public schools in Brooklyn. She was awarded her choice of scholarships but instead of accepting one from well-known and respected Vassar, Shirley agreed that her parents could only afford to send her to Brooklyn College, where she could live at home and save money.

Although this college was for poorer students, its academic requirements were so high that only pupils who went to good high schools would pass the admissions test. The problem with this was that many black students never had the opportunity to "make the grade" because their schools had not overcome the obstacles to learning in poor, black

*Girls High School was an old and respected school for girls in Brooklyn. Shirley St. Hill attended school there from 1939 to 1942.*

areas. As a result, Brooklyn College was 98 percent white.

Shirley knew that her career opportunities were limited simply because she was African American. The fact that she was also a woman further reduced her options. In the 1940s, many doors were closed to

African Americans. Law school and medical school were too expensive (and most would never consider admitting a black woman); doors to other fields, such as sociology or public service, also seemed shut.

The only option left, it seemed, was teaching.

Shirley's interests were varied, and so she took many classes outside of the required education curriculum. Political science was the subject that caught her attention, and it soon developed into a passion. Her first political science professor, a white man named Professor Warsoff, took such an interest in Shirley that they became friends and trusted confidants.

Professor Warsoff taught Shirley that white people are not so different from blacks in that all people share some basic universal emotions, desires, and fears. After hearing her in a debating match, it was Professor Warsoff who first suggested that Shirley put her intelligence and passion to work in politics.

This idea sounded crazy at first. Blacks were not welcome in the college social clubs, and women were never elected to student council. Not deterred, Shirley and some other students formed their own club for African-American women called Ipothia. They chose the name because it stood for "*In pursuit of the highest in all.*"

In her sophomore year, Shirley joined another club, the Harriet Tubman Society, named for the former slave who led other slaves to freedom on the Underground Railroad. This was the only all-black student group at Brooklyn College. Members spent hours debating and discussing ideas about white oppression, black pride, and how to raise racial consciousness. From her discussions with her father and the studying she did on her own, Shirley was well informed yet still naive about America's racial division.

Her eyes were opened from yet another college club, the Political Science Society. This group considered itself quite progressive and invited many speakers and politicians to address the group. What Shirley learned was that these speakers thought that blacks were "limited" in their ability to take care of themselves, so the white establishment felt compelled to help them. In the 1940s, this type of prejudice was a way of life in America.

These tough lessons left their marks on Shirley and her resolve to speak the truth and dispel such myths became very strong. Many people, both black and white, urged her to use her skill and intelligence to pursue some sort of public life. This was difficult praise then for a young woman who wanted both a family and a career. Whether she liked it or not,

*Shirley developed her passion for politics during her years attending Brooklyn College.*

Shirley St. Hill was faced with a difficult reality. Society dictated that women were to be wives and mothers. If she pursued her interests in politics and activism then she would find herself an outcast.

Shirley went to parties in college and enjoyed herself but never dated and made few close friends. Young men found it threatening to date such an intellectual woman who wanted to discuss the issues of the day just as men did.

Whatever might have been lacking in her social life, Shirley made up for in her activism. She joined a number of neighborhood groups outside of the collegiate realm. Each group got a fair chance from Shirley but she was continually disappointed that the organizations seemed content only to talk about problems and rarely took action. The empty words of these groups began to ring in Shirley's ears, making her more determined than ever to make change happen.

Shirley graduated from Brooklyn College in 1946 with honors and set out to get her first teaching job. After many interviews, she was hired as a teacher's aide at the Mt. Calvary Child Care Center in Harlem. Shirley worked there for seven years and moved up through the ranks from teacher's aide to teacher and eventually to become the assistant director.

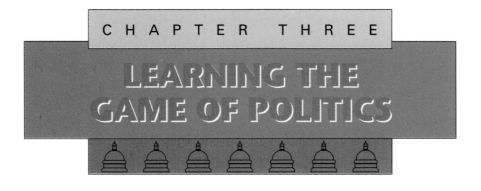

# CHAPTER THREE

# LEARNING THE GAME OF POLITICS

**ALTHOUGH** work was important to Shirley, her first love was politics. She could never understand why the mostly black district of Bedford-Stuyvesant was continually governed by whites. The Democratic Party was the dominant force in New York politics in the 1940s and 1950s, and each voting district had its own political club where people came to discuss political strategies or seek help. During her last year in college, Shirley began to go to the Seventeenth Assembly District Democratic Club meetings and eventually became a valued member. The clubs, however, were run by white men who never dreamed of sharing power with a woman, let alone an African-American woman! The white leadership would sit in the front of the room and look out on a segregated

*Shirley Chisholm in 1971*

audience, blacks on one side and whites on the other. The concepts of racism and sexism were becoming very clear to Shirley as she realized that in some people's eyes, the color of her skin and the fact that she was a woman made her less important and less capable.

Shirley's first appointment was to work with the other women on the club's annual fund-raiser. The money from this event constituted almost the entire budget of the club, which supported the activities of the men. Immediately, Shirley pointed out that the men were taking advantage of the women who were putting all their time and effort into fund-raising but were not allowed to participate in meetings. The other women hadn't thought of this, and when they asked the men for $700 so that they wouldn't have to beg for every cigar box and piece of candy, the men were furious. They branded Shirley a troublemaker (a label she would hear often) and reluctantly gave the women the money. The party was a success and brought in more than $8,000 but little else changed.

Shirley would be told many times in her political career that women should simply follow orders and not expect to play a part in the decision-making process.

In 1946, however, Shirley met an African-American man who encouraged her political activism and never said "a woman can't." Welsey McD.

Holder, or Mac as everyone called him, was never elected to public office (although he tried several times) but he had a great impact on New York politics for several decades. He was a behind-the-scenes player whose main goal was to get blacks elected to government. Shirley was to learn much from Mr. Holder, including getting lessons in understanding the white vs. black and men vs. women politics of the old New York district political clubs.

After working on the successful campaign to elect the first black judge in New York, Shirley stayed under Mr. Holder's guidance and was one of the original members of the Bedford-Stuyvesant Political League (BSPL). The purpose of BSPL was to work toward the election of black candidates at every level of government. Shirley and the other members did whatever had to be done, whether it was door-to-door canvassing or stuffing envelopes for a mailing. No job was too small or unimportant, and Mr. Holder saw to it that Shirley learned how the game of politics was played from every vantage point.

At the same time, Shirley stayed involved in the regular Seventeenth District Assembly Democratic Club and continued working with organizations such as the National Association for the Advancement of Colored People (NAACP) and the League of Women Voters. It was from her work with these groups that Shirley learned what services were desperately needed in the black neighborhoods. But when she would bring up these points at the Democratic Club meetings, she was again branded a troublemaker.

During this time, Shirley also put a great deal of energy into her professional and personal life. She was promoted at Mt. Calvary Child Care Center and later became the head of a 130-pupil child-care center. In 1959, she went to work for the city of New York in its Division of Child Care, where it was her job to visit and evaluate day-care programs across the city.

It was during these years that Shirley got engaged, twice. The first time was to a man she courted for nearly five years but the wedding plans were broken when Shirley discovered that, not only was the man married to a woman in Jamaica, but he was wanted for several immigration scams. Needless to say, Shirley was crushed and resolved that she would never marry.

But along came a quiet and persistent man named Conrad Chisholm. Shirley had decided she was through with men but Conrad continued to pursue her, and eventually she fell in love. With her mother's blessing, Shirley became Mrs. Chisholm in 1949.

Mr. Chisholm was a private investigator who looked into insurance claims. He was a soft-spoken

*Conrad Chisholm pinned a corsage onto his wife's dress in her new office on Capitol Hill after her election to the U.S. House of Representatives. Moments after, Representative Chisholm attended the opening session of the 91st Congress on January 3, 1969.*

man and seemed content to let Mrs. Chisholm have the limelight. In fact, contrary to many people's opinions, Mr. Chisholm was proud of his wife's political fame and was secure enough in his own identity to help her along the way, never seeking the cameras for himself.

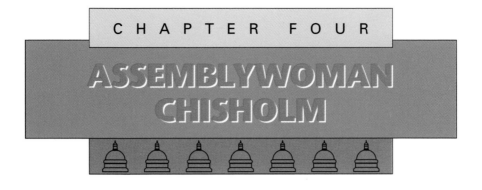

# CHAPTER FOUR

# ASSEMBLYWOMAN CHISHOLM

**SHIRLEY CHISHOLM** decided to form yet another club with five or six colleagues. The Unity Democratic Club began in 1960 with high ideals and a very specific goal: they wanted to get black leaders elected to the New York State Assembly.

This small band did everything they could to get voters' support of their slate of candidates. They even had Eleanor Roosevelt come to New York and campaign for them. But all of their efforts still didn't add up to enough votes.

Instead of throwing in the towel at this point, the Unity Democratic Club set its sights on the election in 1962. Two years of preparation and action from the ground up led them to victory. That year the club's slate won, sending Tom Jones, an African American, to the New York State Assembly. The

*Shirley Chisholm was a familiar sight in her Brooklyn neighbor-hood during her campaigns for both the State Assembly and for the U.S. Congress. She is shown here on her way to a community organization meeting.*

Unity Democratic Club gained a more powerful political voice, but political control still remained in white hands.

Because of some political maneuvering, it was suggested that Tom Jones, after serving only one term, leave his seat in the assembly and run for a judgeship. If he said yes, that would leave an opening for another African American to fill his seat. Shirley thought to herself, After running campaigns for so many men, now it's my turn!

Shirley Chisholm's ten years of stuffing envelopes, ringing doorbells, getting petitions signed, throwing fund-raisers, and helping voters get to the polls always paid off for someone else. Always a man. When Shirley announced her intention to run for the State Assembly she was met with open disdain from black men and women. Many men were threatened by her and many women didn't understand why she would want to do "a man's job." Shirley Chisholm, however, did her best to understand why these people didn't support her.

Still, from her years of working in the community, many people recognized Shirley Chisholm as a leader and someone who would go to the New York State Assembly and fight for them.

Primary elections are held for candidates from the same political party to vie for that party's nomination. The winner of the primary then runs in the general election, where party candidates run against one another. With the Unity Democratic Club's backing, Shirley easily won the primary and went on to win the general election by a wide margin.

Shirley Chisholm's political triumph would have

greatly pleased her father. Unfortunately, he died about a year earlier and did not live to see his eldest daughter become an elected official. Shirley Chisholm and her father were the closest in the family and their common bond was their love of the intellectual and the political. Before her father died, he had made arrangements for some money to be put in Shirley's name but no such arrangements had been made for her sisters. This caused a family rift that was never mended.

★ ★ ★

When Assemblywoman Chisholm arrived in Albany in 1964 (the New York State capital) she found an atmosphere not unlike the old days in the Seventeenth District Assembly Democratic Club. She was one of only six black assembly members and the only black woman. The white men in power made all the rules of the game.

The main focus of the assembly is to consider which bills will become laws. Immediately after a bill is introduced, it is assigned to an appropriate committee, which then analyzes the usefulness and potential effectiveness it will have. This committee also tries to determine how much it will cost, whom it will effect, and how it will be enforced. The bill

*Assemblywoman Chisholm and New York State Senator Basil A. Paterson (left) introduced Julian Bond, a civil rights leader from Atlanta, during his visit to the New York Assembly in January 1965.*

then returns to the full house with a recommendation from the committee's findings either to pass or to defeat it. Often, bills will be assigned to committees, only to join a long list of other bills, each waiting for consideration. Politicians often say "it never got out of committee," which means that the bill sat in line too long and is now "dead" for lack of time or support.

An important component of this process is the "lobbying" effort that representatives and citizens perform. To garner support for a particular bill, interested parties will organize phone calls and letter-writing campaigns to show how many people support or don't support the bill being presented. Because of the volume of bills and varying political stances, a bill must stand out to be recognized as something of some urgency and importance. Representatives work with one another to support projects of their colleagues, usually in return for the support of a bill of their own.

In large legislative bodies such as the New York State Assembly, representatives fall into voting blocs, or groups, that are decided by party membership or by strong personal beliefs. A voting bloc is an important tool because when an assembly member works to get a bill passed, he or she often assumes that if the leadership of a voting bloc will vote for the bill, then all the other votes in that bloc will be cast in the same way. One of the first lessons for a freshman assembly member is learning the consequences of not voting with the bloc that expects her support.

*In 1965, there were only four women in the New York State legislature. Here Assemblywoman Chisholm poses with (from left to right) Assemblywomen Dorothy Rose, Aileen Ryan, and Constance Cook.*

Because Assemblywoman Chisholm was a woman, most of the other representatives assumed that she would go along with the majority bloc on votes of any importance. Shirley Chisholm knew, as did all the other black assembly members, that acting as an individual can cost dearly. Often such "trouble-makers" were assigned to committees that did not work or they would find themselves without any help during the next election.

But from the outset, Assemblywoman Chisholm made her fellow members realize that she was there to get things done — not to just "play the game."

This isn't to say that Assemblywoman Chisholm didn't compromise or work with her fellow legislators. She was quite good at this, as shown by the passage of the eight bills that she introduced. Eight may not sound like a lot, but most representatives introduce as many as fifty or sixty bills each session and only a small percentage of these make it through the complicated process of becoming law.

One of the most important bills Assemblywoman Chisholm got passed was a program named SEEK, which helped young men and women from disadvantaged backgrounds go to college. Another Chisholm bill mandated that personal and domestic workers were entitled to unemployment insurance, and a third bill corrected one of the day's discriminatory practices against women. The assemblywoman's successful bill saw to it that if schoolteachers decided to become pregnant, they would not lose their jobs and seniority when they came back to work.

CHAPTER FIVE

# THE ROAD TO WASHINGTON, D.C.

**SHIRLEY CHISHOLM** learned her lessons well in Albany. So well, in fact, that in 1968, when the opportunity to run for the U.S. Congress presented itself, she was quick to grab it. Because the boundary lines of New York's representative districts were unfair, they were redrawn to make it easier for an African American to represent a district that was largely African American. Plus, the redistricting meant that there were no incumbents or no standing members of Congress who only had to run again among supporters. The field was wide open, and Mrs. Chisholm jumped in with her usual flare and determination.

In this race there were several black candidates who mirrored the racial and ethnic makeup of Bed-Stuy. By sheer numbers, there were more black and

*Representative Chisholm posed with a copy of the* Congressional Record, *the official transcript of all speeches and votes that are given in the U.S. House of Representatives and the Senate.*

Puerto Rican voters than there were white voters. Mrs. Chisholm took note of this and speculated that because of these numbers, she stood a good chance of beating the "establishment" (the white Democratic political bosses), which was backing another candidate.

What she lacked in money and support, Mrs. Chisholm made up for in plain hard work. Her old friend and mentor, Mac Holder, called her up to offer his help. For both of them it was a good match. Mr. Holder had wanted to see his goal of electing an African-American member of Congress, and Mrs. Chisholm wanted to go to Washington to continue what she called "the good fight."

Mr. Holder was the organizer of the campaign and ran the office, making sure the mailing lists were typed, the literature was mailed, and the rallies were put together. Mrs. Chisholm, too, worked long days and especially long weekends. People would see her and her campaign volunteers at the grocery stores handing out bags with her name printed on them. They were also at the clinics and the housing projects and wherever people would listen to what they had to say. While establishment politicians were meeting in back rooms and making plans among only a few, Shirley Chisholm attended house party after house party talking with as many of the voters as she could.

On the weekends, Mrs. Chisholm and her caravan of volunteers could be seen all around the district with banners decorating their cars that read: Fighting Shirley Chisholm — Unbought and Unbossed. This was to let the voters know once and for all that if they sent her to Washington, D.C., she would fight for them and not be manipulated by the powers that be.

After ten months of grueling days and nights of marching up and down the streets talking with as many people as possible, Mrs. Chisholm received her reward. She had become the Democratic Party's candidate after winning the three-way primary election by 1,000 votes. But this didn't mean that she could start packing her bags. It meant only that she had won the first test and now must face another challenger in the general election, this time a Republican African-American candidate named James Farmer. Mr. Farmer was well known as a civil rights leader and had been the national director of the Congress for Racial Equality (CORE).

Before Shirley could begin planning for this next election, tragedy struck. Against her wishes and complaints, Shirley's husband Conrad put his foot down and demanded that she see a doctor about her

*Throughout her political campaigns, Shirley Chisholm's slogan was: "Chisholm — Unbought and Unbossed." Here, supporters during the 1972 Democratic National Convention waved posters and wore hats with the slogan.*

inability to sleep through the night. The doctor took one look at her and explained that Shirley had a tumor growing in her pelvic area. Luckily, the growth was not cancerous but the doctors were adamant that it still be removed.

In her usual fashion, Shirley argued and argued that she couldn't take time out from her campaign for the operation and asked why it couldn't just wait until November. But Conrad Chisholm and the doctors persisted and left her no choice. The operation was swift and without any complications. The difficult part for Shirley was the time needed to heal.

For almost six weeks she was kept in bed. She had lost a lot of weight, and it took several weeks for her to get her strength back. But once Shirley Chisholm had decided that she had stayed out of the congressional race long enough, there was no stopping her.

Even though she had a great amount of energy and grassroots support, James Farmer had been busy all those weeks Shirley Chisholm spent getting well, and every minor mistake was magnified into a crisis. Mac Holder, realizing that a more full-time effort was needed, turned all of his attention to running every detail of the campaign, leaving his candidate free to talk directly with the voters. Mac Holder was especially helpful when it came to strategizing.

The winning strategy evolved when Farmer began criticizing Shirley Chisholm's abilities and intelligence. Farmer also emphasized that Mrs. Chisholm was a woman. He thought that he could capitalize on the opinions of the day that regulated the strict guidelines of "women's work" and "men's work." "Government," said Farmer, "was a man's job."

*James Farmer, a nationally known figure, was Shirley Chisholm's Republican opponent in the 1968 race to be New York's 12th District congressperson.*

But Mac Holder had done his research and learned that women voters outnumbered men voters in that district. Shirley Chisholm immediately knew that she had to get the women of the PTA and the bridge clubs behind her, for these were the people who had witnessed firsthand her work and commitment to bettering their lives. The rest of the needed support would follow. So when Farmer raised the issue of gender as a negative, it worked against him. Mr. Holder and Mrs. Chisholm discovered that being a woman was one of her greatest assets.

Another of Shirley Chisholm's strengths was her ability to speak Spanish fluently. She had studied the language in college and was able to communicate with the thousands of Spanish-speaking voters in their own language. Where Farmer had a great barrier to cross, Mrs. Chisholm had no problems communicating her message correctly and directly.

The strategies and hard work paid off on election day. Shirley Chisholm beat James Farmer by a $2\frac{1}{2}$ to 1 margin. In January 1969, she was sworn into the U.S. House of Representatives, the first African-American woman to achieve such a position. At this time there were only eight other African-American members of Congress (all of them men) and only ten other women.

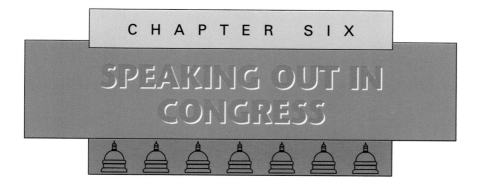

# CHAPTER SIX

# SPEAKING OUT IN CONGRESS

**THE U.S. HOUSE** of Representatives, together with the Senate, is the nation's largest legislative body. There are 435 members of the House of Representatives and each must follow a long list of rules and protocol that have developed over the years. Those members with the most seniority are the ones who control the most power. For instance, every congressperson must sit on a committee in addition to voting on bills and assisting the constituents of his or her district. In 1969, the committee assignments were doled out by the congressional leadership who met behind closed doors. If new members of Congress didn't like their committee assignment, congressional protocol said that they must "be good soldiers" and wait

*Representative Chisholm stands on the steps of the Capitol before her famous speech against the Vietnam War in spring 1969. She said, "Unless we start to fight and defeat the enemies in our own country, poverty and racism, and make our talk of equality and opportunity ring true, we are exposed in the eyes of the world as hypocrites when we talk about making people free."*

patiently until they built enough seniority to have a say in the matter.

This scenario did not play well for Congresswoman Chisholm. In her first few weeks in Washington, she broke some major rules and decided to risk her political future by speaking out.

Congresswoman Chisholm's years in teaching and education made her a natural for the Education and Labor Committee. But it was a long shot to get her first choice of committee assignments. Failing that assignment, Congresswoman Chisholm drew up a long list of other committees to which she could contribute and help the people back home.

When the committees were announced, Congresswoman Chisholm learned, to her horror, that she had been placed on the Agriculture Committee. This was not an interest for her, but she recognized that even on this committee she could make a difference because it had jurisdiction over such programs as food stamps and surplus food distribution. The blow came when Congresswoman Chisholm was assigned to the Forestry and Rural Development subcommittees. There was no way she could pretend that these two subcommittees would have much to do with the poor black, Hispanic, and white people in Bedford-Stuyvesant.

What the congresswoman did next was unthinkable! She called the Speaker of the House John McCormick and explained her predicament. Speaker McCormick listened and then explained that Mrs. Chisholm would just have to put in her time and maybe in a few years she would get a better assignment. After Shirley Chisholm protested more, the Speaker agreed to see what he could do but Con-

*Although Shirley Chisholm was officially sworn into Congress along with the other new members in a ceremony on the House floor, Speaker of the House John McCormick administered the oath of office to her again in a private gathering.*

gresswoman Chisholm decided that she had no choice but to go to the floor.

There is a formality that requires the committee assignments to be passed by a majority of Congress. Shirley Chisholm could bring her issue to the floor and appeal to the other members to change her assignment. But before she could do that, the congresswoman had to "be recognized."

When one wants to address the House, he or she must be formally recognized by the Speaker to take a turn at the microphone. Traditionally, the Speaker recognizes the more senior members of Congress. Congresswoman Chisholm was not surprised when, every time she rose to be recognized, several other senior members rose, too. Finally, Congresswoman Chisholm left her seat and marched down to the microphone in front of the Speaker so that he had no choice but to let her speak.

After a brief speech, Congresswoman Chisholm introduced a resolution that would have her reassigned. It passed, and a few weeks later Shirley Chisholm reported to the Veterans Affairs Committee. It wasn't her first choice, but it was certainly a step in the right direction. As Congresswoman Chisholm noted, "There are a lot more veterans in my district than trees!"

It is not hard to imagine how this skinny African-

American woman from New York upset the time-honored sleepy movement of the House. Again she was labeled a troublemaker and one to watch. Even the press debated her actions, and although many newspapers noted that Congresswoman Chisholm was correct in challenging the old ways, some reporters condemned her for not waiting her turn and spending years building clout as did everyone else.

Being called a troublemaker and having some obstacles thrown in your path is never pleasant, but at least it means you are being heard. The question now for Congresswoman Chisholm was exactly what *did* she want to say. She chose to focus her efforts around two major themes (in addition to attending to the core of her work as a member of Congress): Be a leader for women and African Americans across the country.

Although she made headlines with her maiden speech (the first speech given in Congress by a freshman legislator) about opposing more money for the Vietnam War, Congresswoman Chisholm went to Washington, D.C., to fight for jobs, education, enforcement for antidiscrimination laws, and other social issues. It was on these matters that she spent much time and energy. Equal rights for women was another rallying cry for the congresswoman. Once again, Shirley Chisholm made headlines when she came out in support of repealing the anti-abortion laws. She felt very strongly that no one should be forced to have an abortion, but she knew that abortion was a leading cause of death for nonwhite women in the 1960s because unsafe procedures were followed

*The nine African-American members of Congress in 1970 formed the "black bloc," that is now known as the Black Congressional Caucus. Representative Chisholm is shown here in 1974 with Representative Charles Rangle, also from a district in New York, as leaders of the caucus following a meeting with President Gerald R. Ford.*

in illegal operations. At the same time, Mrs. Chisholm also campaigned for more day-care centers and better working conditions for women and mothers.

Congresswoman Chisholm joined with other female legislators to work toward equal rights for women, and she was a sponsor of the Equal Rights Amendment, which would have outlawed discrimination on the basis of sex. (Although this amendment to the Constitution was passed in Congress in 1970, it was never ratified by enough state legislatures to make it into law.)

Because she had been the first African-American woman to be elected to Congress, Mrs. Chisholm was an instant national celebrity. She received hundreds of invitations to speak at all kinds of gatherings and was especially popular on college campuses. Her speeches were a call to action for students to get involved in what was happening in America. She urged the students to "ask questions and demand answers . . . you must live in the mainstream of your time and of your generation."

The first four years Shirley Chisholm spent in Congress were a wealth of experience and education. Toward the end of 1971, the idea of reaching for a higher goal began to develop, and Mrs. Chisholm soon found herself declaring her candidacy for the Democratic presidential nomination. From her national speaking engagements, the congresswoman had excellent name recognition and was continually encouraged to run for president every time she visited another college campus.

The Democratic Convention was to be held in August 1972, and it would be there that the party's nominee would be chosen to run against the incumbent, President Richard M. Nixon. Shirley Chisholm and other black leaders knew that if they were to ever assert their political power, they would need to show their strength at the convention.

But even among African-American political leaders personal ambitions and individual strategies collided, and a consensus could not be reached as to how to approach the convention. Consequently, differing factions arose, and Mrs. Chisholm assessed early on that she could not count on their support. Even more than personal ambitions, the other black politicians (almost all men) refused to throw their votes behind a woman. Shirley Chisholm found herself in the middle of two minorities, neither of which would help her obtain her goal.

The campaign moved onward and Mrs. Chisholm ran in several state primaries to gauge what percentage of the votes she could attract. There were no delusions that Congresswoman Chisholm would actually win any of the primaries. She just wanted to

*The sign says it all! Representative Chisholm announced her campaign to run for president of the United States in February 1972.*

help the progress of women and African Americans, and by staying in the public spotlight and talking about the "good fight," she could do just that. Every time Shirley Chisholm appeared at a rally or on the news she served as a reminder of the millions of women and African Americans who were ready to use their votes to elect a leader that would address their needs.

But inexperience and the lack of money reared their ugly heads and caused many rifts. There was little money to spend and almost all of the campaign workers were volunteers. Because Mrs. Chisholm was slow in appointing a campaign manager to coordinate and prioritize activities, many clashes erupted. Women in the campaign argued over strategy with African-American volunteers, and the two groups acted more like warring factions than team players. Mrs. Chisholm realized too late that she did not have enough time to campaign across the country, continue her work as a congressperson, and heal the anger and hurt feelings among her campaign staff.

After six months of campaigning, the last leg of this journey began with the opening of the Democratic Convention. Mrs. Chisholm lobbied the black delegates hard to support her at least on the first ballot. Everyone knew that there would not be enough votes to actually win but Mrs. Chisholm was firm in

*At the 1972 Democratic National Convention, Shirley Chisholm congratulates George McGovern on winning the presidential nomination.*

her belief that America's women, African Americans, poor, and underrepresented deserved some public recognition.

Her pleas were answered, but it was too late. George McGovern had been nominated, and Mrs. Chisholm faded into the background until the convention's end.

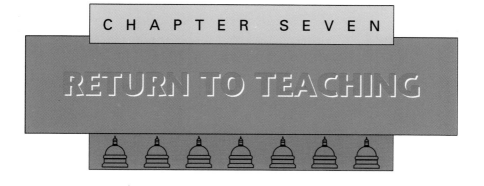

# CHAPTER SEVEN

# RETURN TO TEACHING

**WITH THE PRESIDENTIAL** election behind her, Mrs. Chisholm returned to the business of being a congresswoman until 1982, when she retired to return to an earlier love, teaching and lecturing.

After delivering a graduating speech at Mt. Holyoke College, Shirley Chisholm was asked to come back to the college to teach several courses. She enjoyed teaching greatly and was a professor at Mt. Holyoke until she moved to Florida to teach at the well-known black school, Spelman College.

Mrs. Chisholm also continued to be active in politics, although she did not seek any other elected office for herself. In 1985, the National Political Congress of Black Women was created, with Shirley Chisholm as the first president. The group was orga-

*Representative Chisholm in her Brooklyn office in 1982.*

nized because the concerns and the political careers
of African-American women seemed to be ignored at
the 1984 Democratic National Convention. Once
again, Shirley Chisholm was at the forefront of social

change and the advancement of African-American women.

Today, Shirley Chisholm keeps a low profile but still remains active in politics and is writing a book. In a Spelman College address, Mrs. Chisholm once said, "Success comes from doing to the best of your ability what you know in your heart are the right things to do."

This is advice Shirley Chisholm has followed her whole life and she has been, without a doubt, successful.

# FOR FURTHER READING

Chisholm, Shirley. *Unbought and Unbossed*. Boston: Houghton Mifflin Company, 1970.

Haskins, James. *Fighting Shirley Chisholm*. New York: Dial Press, 1975.

Hicks, Nancy. *The Honorable Shirley Chisholm, Congresswoman from Brooklyn*. New York: Lion Books, 1971.

McKissack, Patricia, and Fredrick McKissack. *The Civil Rights Movement in America from 1865 to the Present*. 2d ed. Chicago: Childrens Press, 1991.

Scheader, Catherine. *Shirley Chisholm, Teacher & Congresswoman*. New Jersey: Enslow Publishing, 1990.

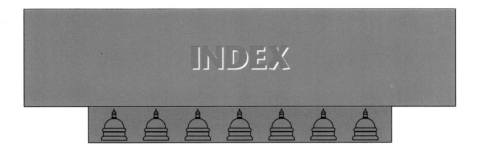

# INDEX

Page numbers in *italics* refer to illustrations

# ABOUT THE AUTHOR

**JILL S. POLLACK** is a writer and editor whose work has appeared in newspapers, magazines, trade periodicals, and political journals. A graduate of The George Washington University, Ms. Pollack has worked on political campaigns and with political action committees, and is currently writing a book about women in national politics. She lives in Chicago.